All About Dolphins

Fascinating Facts and Cool Information
Guaranteed to Blow Your Mind

MENTAL BOMB PUBLISHING

INTRODUCTION

Embark on a journey through the fascinating and awe-inspiring world of dolphins. Brace yourself for a tidal wave of incredible information about these amazing creatures.

Did you know that dolphins have been known to form lifelong friendships, displaying a level of social intelligence that rivals our own? Dive deep into the oceanic depths as we uncover the secrets of their intricate communication, their unparalleled problem-solving abilities, and the playful games that make them the true acrobats of the sea.

Prepare to be amazed by their extraordinary senses, from echolocation that rivals a superhero's radar to their finely tuned sonar, allowing them to navigate the ocean with unparalleled precision.

Explore the various dolphin species, from the charismatic bottlenose dolphins to the dazzling spinner dolphins, each with its own unique traits.

So, flip open the pages, immerse yourself in the wonders of the deep, and enjoy the incredible world of these aquatic marvels!

All About Dolphins

MENTAL BOMB
Our goal is to entertain and to blow your mind!

Visit us online at MentalBomb.com
Home for the best illusions, riddles, games, and fun facts!

Follow

Facebook: Mental-Bomb-
Instagram: mental_bomb_
Pinterest: Mental_Bomb
Twitter: MentalBomb_

CONTENTS

1. What Are Dolphins?

Dolphins are remarkable marine mammals renowned for their intelligence, social complexity, and remarkable agility. Belonging to the order Cetacea, they share this classification with whales and porpoises, collectively forming a diverse group of aquatic mammals. With their sleek, streamlined bodies, dolphins are well-adapted to life in the water. They typically feature a dorsal fin on their back, a horizontally-oriented tail fin, and a layer of blubber beneath their skin to insulate them in varying ocean temperatures.

These highly intelligent creatures exhibit a level of cognitive ability that is among the most advanced in the animal kingdom. Dolphins possess the capacity for complex problem-solving, learning through observation, and even using tools. Their communication skills are equally impressive, relying on a diverse range of vocalizations, including clicks, whistles, and body movements. In addition, dolphins demonstrate self-awareness, a trait few species share, further highlighting their cognitive sophistication.

Socially, dolphins are known for their strong bonds and cooperative behavior within tightly-knit groups known as pods. These pods vary in size and composition, with some consisting of only a few individuals while others comprise several hundred. Communication within pods is intricate, involving a nuanced system of sounds and body language. These social structures contribute to the well-being and survival of individual dolphins within the group, fostering shared responsibilities in tasks such as hunting and protecting each other from predators.

Dolphins are primarily carnivorous, with their diet consisting mainly of fish and squid. Some species are known for their cooperative hunting strategies, where individuals collaborate to corral and capture prey. Despite being marine creatures, dolphins must come to the water's surface regularly to breathe. They possess a blowhole located on the top of their heads, allowing for efficient inhalation of air. This adaptation, along with their streamlined bodies and powerful tails, enables dolphins to navigate their oceanic habitats with remarkable speed and agility.

Found in oceans and seas worldwide, dolphins inhabit a range of environments, from coastal waters to deep oceanic expanses. Some species, like the bottlenose dolphin, are well-known for their playful interactions with humans, captivating people around the world. As fascinating inhabitants of our oceans, dolphins contribute to the balance of marine ecosystems and continue to be subjects of scientific study, conservation efforts, and public admiration.

The following are several defining characteristics and critical facts about dolphins:

1. **Physical Features**: Dolphins typically have streamlined bodies, a dorsal fin on their back, and a horizontally-oriented tail fin. They have a layer of blubber to insulate them in cold water.

2. **Intelligence**: Dolphins are known for their high level of intelligence. They are capable of complex problem-solving, learning through observation, and using tools. They also exhibit self-awareness.

3. **Social Behavior**: Dolphins are highly social animals and often live in groups called pods. These pods can vary in size, ranging from a few individuals to several hundred. Social bonds within pods are strong, and dolphins communicate through a variety of vocalizations and body language.

4. **Communication**: Dolphins use a range of vocalizations, including clicks, whistles, and body movements, to communicate with each other. They have sophisticated echolocation abilities, using sound waves to navigate and locate prey.

5. **Diet**: Dolphins are carnivores, and their diet primarily consists of fish and squid. Some species are known for cooperative hunting strategies, where they work together to corral and capture prey.

6. **Habitat**: Dolphins are found in oceans and seas around the world, although some species inhabit freshwater rivers and estuaries. They are adapted to a wide range of environments, from coastal waters to deep oceanic areas.

7. **Breathing**: Dolphins are mammals, so they breathe air. They have a blowhole located on the top of their heads, and they must come to the surface regularly to breathe.

8. **Reproduction**: Female dolphins give birth to live young, and the calf is typically cared for by its mother and other members of the pod. The gestation period varies by species.

2. Dolphin Evolution

The evolutionary history of dolphins is a fascinating tale of adaptation and transformation that spans tens of millions of years. Dolphins, along with whales and porpoises, are members of the cetacean order, and their journey from land to sea reveals remarkable changes in form and function.

The roots of dolphin evolution trace back to terrestrial ancestors that lived around 50 to 55 million years ago. These early mammals gradually transitioned to an aquatic lifestyle, and the fossil record provides evidence of this process. Ambulocetus and protocetids were among the first cetaceans that displayed some aquatic adaptations while retaining features suited for life on land. The gradual shift from limbs capable of walking to more streamlined bodies with elongated tails marked a critical phase in cetacean evolution.

The emergence of basilosaurids around 40 million years ago represented a significant milestone. These ancient whales showcased more advanced adaptations to aquatic life, with elongated bodies and the presence of tail flukes. While not direct ancestors of modern dolphins, basilosaurids played a crucial role in the evolutionary trajectory toward streamlined, fully aquatic forms.

By around 25 to 30 million years ago, the divergence of odontocetes, including dolphins, from baleen whales marked a key evolutionary branching point. This period saw the development of echolocation, a sophisticated sensory adaptation that remains a hallmark of odontocete evolution. The evolution of echolocation provided dolphins with a powerful tool for navigating their underwater environments, communicating with one another, and locating prey.

The subsequent 10 million years witnessed the emergence of dolphin species closely resembling their modern counterparts during the Miocene epoch. These early dolphins continued to diversify, adapting to different ecological niches and evolving into the diverse array of species we recognize today. The evolution of dolphins is a testament to the remarkable ability of life to adapt and thrive in varied environments, ultimately resulting in the intelligent, social, and acrobatic marine mammals we marvel at in the world's oceans.

The following are some amazing facts about dolphin evolution:

1. **Land Ancestors:** Dolphins, despite their aquatic lifestyle, share a common ancestry with terrestrial mammals. The ancestors of dolphins were land-dwelling mammals that gradually transitioned to life in the water over millions of years.

2. **Eocene Epoch Transition:** The critical transition from land to water occurred during the Eocene epoch, approximately 50 to 55 million years ago. This period saw the emergence of early cetaceans with adaptations for both terrestrial and aquatic environments.

3. **Ambulocetus and Protocetids**: Ambulocetus and protocetids were early cetaceans that retained some features of land mammals, including limbs capable of both walking and swimming. These creatures represent key stages in the evolutionary journey toward fully aquatic forms.

4. **Basilosaurids and Streamlined Bodies**: The basilosaurids, appearing around 40 million years ago, displayed more advanced adaptations to aquatic life. They had elongated bodies and tail flukes, marking a significant shift toward the streamlined form characteristic of modern dolphins.

5. **Divergence from Baleen Whales**: Around 25 to 30 million years ago, odontocetes, the group that includes dolphins, diverged from baleen whales. This divergence marked a crucial point in cetacean evolution, leading to the development of features such as echolocation, which is a key adaptation for dolphins.

6. **Evolution of Echolocation**: The evolution of echolocation, a sophisticated sensory adaptation, occurred within the odontocete lineage. Echolocation allows dolphins to navigate their underwater surroundings, communicate with each other, and locate prey using sound waves.

7. **Miocene Epoch and Modern Dolphin Resemblance**: During the Miocene epoch, around 10 million years ago, dolphin species closely resembling modern forms began to emerge. This period marked a significant step in the evolution of the diverse array of dolphin species we recognize today.

8. **Variety of Environments**: Dolphins have adapted to a wide range of environments, from coastal waters to deep oceanic expanses. This adaptability is reflected in the diversity of species, each suited to specific ecological niches.

9. **Social Complexity:** Over the course of evolution, dolphins developed highly social behaviors. They form complex social structures within pods, demonstrating strong social bonds, cooperation in hunting, and communication through a variety of vocalizations.

10. **Cognitive Sophistication:** The evolution of dolphins is marked by a notable increase in cognitive abilities. Dolphins are among the most intelligent animals on Earth, exhibiting problem-solving skills, self-awareness, and the ability to learn through observation and interaction.

3. Dolphin Diversity

Dolphins display remarkable diversity in terms of species, size, distribution, and behavior. They belong to the family Delphinidae within the order Cetacea, and the following are some common categories and examples of dolphins:

1. **Bottlenose Dolphins (Genus Tursiops):** Perhaps the most well-known group, bottlenose dolphins are characterized by their distinctive short, stubby rostrum or beak. The common bottlenose dolphin (Tursiops truncatus) is widely recognized and often featured in marine parks. They are found in both coastal and offshore waters globally.

2. **Oceanic Dolphins (Delphinidae Family):** This broad category includes various species of dolphins inhabiting open ocean environments. Examples include the common dolphin (Delphinus delphis), which encompasses both the short-beaked common dolphin and the long-beaked common dolphin. Oceanic dolphins are known for their acrobatic displays and are found in warm and temperate seas.

3. **River Dolphins (Various Genera):** Some dolphins have adapted to freshwater environments and are referred to as river dolphins. Examples include the Amazon River Dolphin (Inia geoffrensis) found in South America and the Ganges River Dolphin (Platanista gangetica) in parts of South Asia. River dolphins often have longer snouts and different physical adaptations compared to their marine counterparts.

4. **Porpoises (Phocoenidae Family):** While not dolphins, porpoises are closely related and often mentioned alongside them. Porpoises include species like the harbor porpoise (Phocoena phocoena). They are generally smaller than dolphins, have a more robust body, and lack the prominent beak seen in many dolphins.

5. **Spinner Dolphins (Genus Stenella):** Spinner dolphins, such as the spinner dolphin (Stenella longirostris), are known for their acrobatic spins and leaps. They are found in tropical and subtropical waters and are often associated with offshore environments.

6. **Killer Whales or Orcas (Orcinus orca):** While commonly referred to as whales, orcas are actually the largest members of the dolphin family. They are highly intelligent and are known for their complex social structures, distinctive black and white coloring, and diverse diet that can include fish, seals, and even other whales.

7. **False Killer Whales (Pseudorca crassidens):** Another species often mentioned alongside dolphins, the false killer whale, is a large and powerful cetacean. Despite its name, it is not closely related to killer whales. False killer whales are found in tropical and temperate seas worldwide.

These categories represent just a fraction of the diverse world of dolphins. The various species within these categories exhibit adaptations to specific environments, social structures, and behaviors, contributing to the rich tapestry of marine life in oceans and rivers across the globe.

4. Dolphin Biology

Dolphin biology is a testament to the remarkable adaptations that enable these marine mammals to thrive in their aquatic habitats. Dolphins belong to the order Cetacea, specifically the family Delphinidae, and are characterized by their streamlined bodies, which are well-suited for efficient swimming. Their skin is smooth and rubbery, lacking sweat glands, and they maintain their body temperature through countercurrent heat exchange and adjustments in surface-to-volume ratio. A layer of blubber beneath their skin serves as insulation and buoyancy, aiding in thermal regulation and providing additional buoyancy for efficient swimming.

Respiration is a crucial aspect of dolphin biology. Dolphins are conscious breathers, meaning they actively come to the water's surface to breathe through a blowhole located on the top of their heads. This adaptation allows them to remain submerged for varying durations while engaging in activities such as hunting or socializing. Dolphins also possess well-developed eyes adapted for both aquatic and aerial vision. Their vision is crucial for locating prey and navigating in different light conditions.

One of the most distinctive features of dolphin biology is their echolocation ability. Dolphins emit clicks, and by analyzing the echoes of these clicks, they can navigate their environment, locate prey, and communicate with other dolphins. The melon, a fatty structure in their forehead, plays a crucial role in focusing and directing these clicks. Dolphins are toothed whales, and their teeth are adapted for grasping and catching prey rather than chewing. They typically swallow their prey whole.

Dolphins exhibit exceptional hearing capabilities, allowing them to perceive a broad range of frequencies. Their complex auditory system is vital for communication within pods and for interpreting the echoes in their echolocation process. Furthermore, dolphins have relatively large and complex brains, particularly the neocortex, associated with advanced cognitive functions. This high level of intelligence is evident in their problem-solving abilities, learning through observation, and the development of complex social structures.

Socially, dolphins are highly interactive and form pods, exhibiting strong social bonds. Communication within these pods involves a diverse range of vocalizations and body language, contributing to their cooperative behaviors in activities such as hunting and protection from predators. Understanding the intricacies of dolphin biology not only sheds light on their evolutionary journey but also underscores the importance of conservation efforts to safeguard these intelligent and socially complex marine mammals.

The following summarizes the key aspects of dolphin biology:

1. **Body Structure**: Dolphins have a streamlined body shape, which is well-adapted for efficient swimming. They typically have a fusiform body, a dorsal fin on their back, and a horizontal tail fluke that propels them through the water. The absence of hind limbs contributes to their streamlined form.

2. **Skin**: Dolphin skin is smooth and rubbery. It lacks sweat glands, so they maintain their body temperature through other means, such as countercurrent heat exchange in blood vessels and surface-to-volume ratio adjustments.

3. **Blubber**: Like many marine mammals, dolphins have a layer of blubber beneath their skin. Blubber serves as insulation, helping them regulate body temperature in cold water and providing buoyancy.

4. **Respiration**: Dolphins are mammals, and they breathe air. They have a blowhole located on the top of their heads, and they must come to the water's surface regularly to breathe. Dolphins are conscious breathers, meaning they have to actively come to the surface to take each breath.

5. **Echolocation**: Dolphins are known for their sophisticated echolocation abilities. They emit clicks and listen to the echoes to navigate their environment, locate prey, and communicate with other dolphins. The complex structure of their melon (a fatty organ in their forehead) aids in focusing and directing these clicks.

6. **Teeth**: Dolphins are toothed whales, and their teeth are designed for grasping and catching prey. While the number of teeth varies among species, they typically have a set of conical teeth that are not used for chewing. Instead, dolphins swallow their prey whole.

7. **Vision**: Dolphins have well-developed eyes and can see both in and out of the water. Their eyes are adapted to low light conditions, aiding them in locating prey and navigating in the ocean depths.

8. **Hearing**: Dolphins have excellent hearing abilities, crucial for their communication and echolocation. They can hear a broad range of frequencies, and their ears are adapted to receive sounds both in and out of the water.

9. **Brain**: Dolphins have relatively large and complex brains compared to their body size. They are known for their high level of intelligence and cognitive abilities. The neocortex, associated with higher functions such as problem-solving and self-awareness, is particularly well-developed in dolphins.

10. **Social Structure**: Dolphins are highly social animals, often forming groups called pods. Social bonds within pods are strong, and they communicate through a variety of vocalizations and body language. Cooperative behaviors, such as hunting and protecting each other from predators, are common within pods.

5. Where Dolphins Live – Habitats

Dolphins are highly adaptable marine mammals, and they inhabit a wide range of aquatic environments around the world. The specific species and their distribution can vary, but generally, dolphins can be found in the following habitats:

1. **Oceans:** Dolphins are widespread in the world's oceans and can be found in both coastal and offshore waters. Different species may have preferences for specific oceanic regions, and they may range from the Arctic and Antarctic to tropical and temperate waters.

2. **Seas:** Dolphins inhabit various seas, including the Mediterranean Sea, the Red Sea, the Arabian Sea, and others. The specific species present in each sea can vary based on factors such as water temperature, prey availability, and other environmental conditions.

3. **Gulf and Bays:** Dolphins are often found in the sheltered waters of gulfs and bays. These areas can provide abundant food sources and protection for dolphins and their calves. Examples include the Gulf of Mexico, the Bay of Biscay, and Shark Bay in Australia.

4. **Estuaries and River Mouths:** Some species of dolphins, known as river dolphins, inhabit estuarine and riverine environments. Examples include the Amazon River Dolphin and the Ganges River Dolphin. These dolphins have adapted to both saltwater and freshwater conditions.

5. **Rivers:** While most dolphins are marine, a few species, like the Amazon River Dolphin, can be found in freshwater rivers and tributaries. These dolphins have adapted to life in rivers and are known as freshwater or river dolphins.

6. **Coastlines:** Dolphins are commonly seen along coastlines, where they may engage in feeding, socializing, and traveling. Coastal areas provide a mix of habitats and are often rich in prey.

7. **Pelagic Waters:** Some species of dolphins, such as the common dolphin and the spinner dolphin, are known as pelagic dolphins and are frequently found in deep offshore waters. They often travel in large groups and are known for their acrobatic displays.

6. Dolphin Intelligence

Dolphin intelligence is widely recognized as exceptional among non-human animals. These marine mammals exhibit a range of cognitive abilities that demonstrate complex thinking, problem-solving, social awareness, and communication skills.

Here are some key aspects of dolphin intelligence:

1. **Encephalization:** Dolphins have relatively large brains compared to their body size. The neocortex, a region associated with higher cognitive functions, is particularly well-developed in dolphins. This encephalization is an indicator of advanced cognitive capabilities.

2. **Problem-Solving Skills:** Dolphins are known for their ability to solve problems and adapt to changing situations. They can learn from experience, apply knowledge gained in one context to another, and devise strategies for obtaining food or overcoming challenges.

3. **Tool Use:** While not as extensively documented as in some other species, there is evidence that dolphins engage in tool use. For example, bottlenose dolphins in Shark Bay, Australia, use sponges to protect their rostrums while foraging on the seafloor.

4. **Self-Awareness:** Dolphins exhibit signs of self-awareness, a trait shared by only a few species, including humans and great apes. Mirror tests have demonstrated that dolphins can recognize themselves in a mirror, indicating a level of self-awareness.

5. **Communication and Vocalization:** Dolphins are highly vocal and use a complex system of clicks, whistles, and body language for communication. They have signature whistles, unique to each individual, which may serve as a form of individual identification within a pod. The intricacy of their communication suggests a high level of social intelligence.

6. **Echolocation:** Dolphins use echolocation for navigation, communication, and hunting. This sophisticated sensory ability involves emitting clicks and interpreting the returning echoes to perceive their surroundings. The precision of their echolocation contributes to their success in finding prey and avoiding obstacles.

7. **Social Structure:** Dolphins live in social groups called pods, and their social structure is intricate. They engage in cooperative behaviors such as hunting, herding prey, and protecting one another. Long-lasting social bonds exist within pods, and individuals may exhibit empathy and cooperation.

8. **Playfulness:** Dolphins are known for their playful behaviors, which include leaping, riding waves, and playing with objects. Play is considered a sign of intelligence and is thought to contribute to social bonding and cognitive development.

9. **Cultural Transmission:** Some dolphin populations exhibit cultural behaviors passed down through generations. This can include specific hunting techniques, vocalizations, and even forms of play. The ability to transmit and maintain cultural knowledge is indicative of cognitive complexity.

Dolphin intelligence is a subject of ongoing research, and scientists continue to explore the depth of their cognitive abilities. The combination of problem-solving skills, social complexity, communication abilities, and other cognitive traits makes dolphins one of the most intellectually advanced species in the animal kingdom.

7. Echolocation

Echolocation is a biological sonar system used by some animals, including dolphins, to navigate their environment, locate prey, and communicate with others. It involves emitting sounds, usually in the form of clicks, and then interpreting the returning echoes to gather information about the surrounding objects.

Here's how dolphins use echolocation:

1. **Sound Emission:** Dolphins produce high-frequency clicks, which are often beyond the range of human hearing. These clicks are generated in the nasal passages, and the sound waves are directed into the water through the dolphin's lower jaw. The clicks are then emitted into the surrounding environment.

2. **Propagation of Sound Waves:** The clicks travel through the water, and when they encounter an object or a boundary between different substances (like water and air), they are partially reflected back as echoes.

3. **Reception of Echoes:** The echoes are detected by the dolphin's lower jaw, which contains specialized structures called the lower jaw complex. These structures transmit the received sounds to the dolphin's inner ear.

4. **Interpretation of Echoes:** The dolphin's brain processes the information from the returning echoes, allowing the dolphin to create a mental map of its surroundings. The time it takes for the echo to return provides information about the distance to the

object, while the frequency shift (Doppler effect) can indicate the relative motion of the object.

5. **Precise Targeting:** Dolphins are capable of extremely precise targeting using echolocation. They can discern the size, shape, and even the internal structure of objects, helping them navigate through complex underwater environments, locate prey, and avoid obstacles.

6. **Adaptation to Different Environments:** Dolphins can adjust the frequency, intensity, and pattern of their clicks based on their environment. In open water, where echoes are more straightforward, they may use higher-frequency clicks. In more complex environments, like near the seafloor, they might use lower-frequency clicks to obtain clearer echoes.

Echolocation is a crucial skill for dolphins, especially when hunting. They use it to locate and identify prey species, determine the size and shape of fish schools, and even detect individual fish hidden in sand or mud. Dolphins can also use echolocation to communicate with other members of their pod, as they can produce clicks that carry specific information.

8. Dolphin Social Structures

Dolphins are known for their complex and dynamic social structures, and their social behavior is a defining characteristic of their species. Here are key features of dolphin social structures:

1. **Pods:** The fundamental social unit for dolphins is the pod, a group of individuals that live and travel together. Pods vary in size, with some consisting of just a few individuals, while others can comprise several dozen members. The size and composition of pods can change over time, with individuals joining or leaving for various reasons.

2. **Family Bonds:** Within a pod, family bonds are strong. Mother-calf relationships are particularly important, with calves staying close to their mothers for an extended period. Other close familial relationships may exist between siblings and extended family members.

3. **Cooperative Behaviors:** Dolphins are highly cooperative animals, and pod members work together in various activities. This cooperation is evident in hunting, where dolphins coordinate to corral and capture prey. Cooperative behaviors also extend to activities such as herding schools of fish, protecting vulnerable members of the pod, and even playing together.

4. **Communication:** Communication is a vital component of dolphin social structures. Dolphins use a sophisticated system of vocalizations, including clicks, whistles, and body language, to convey information. Each dolphin has a unique signature whistle, and individuals within a pod can recognize and call each other by these distinctive vocalizations.

5. **Social Bonds Beyond Family:** While family bonds are crucial, dolphins also form strong social bonds beyond immediate family

members. These bonds contribute to the cohesion of the pod and facilitate cooperative behaviors. Long-lasting relationships may exist between non-related individuals within the pod.

6. **Alliances and Subgroups:** Within larger pods, smaller subgroups or alliances may form. These subgroups can consist of individuals with common interests or affiliations. Such alliances may be particularly evident during activities like hunting or socializing.

7. **Play and Socializing:** Dolphins engage in play as a form of socializing and bonding. Playful behaviors include leaping, riding waves, playing with objects, and engaging in social games. Play is not only a means of building social bonds but also serves as a way for dolphins to practice and develop skills.

8. **Cohesiveness:** The cohesiveness of dolphin pods contributes to the overall success and survival of individual members. Cooperative hunting, protection from predators, and shared parenting responsibilities are facilitated by the strong social bonds within the pod.

9. **Empathy and Support:** Observations suggest that dolphins may exhibit empathy and support for one another. Injured or distressed individuals may receive assistance from pod members, and there are instances of dolphins supporting each other during times of vulnerability.

Dolphin social structures vary among species and populations, and researchers continue to study these behaviors to gain deeper insights into the complexity of dolphin societies. The cooperative and communicative nature of their social structures is a key factor in the adaptability and success of dolphins in a variety of marine environments.

9. Dolphin Parenthood

Dolphin reproduction involves distinctive behaviors, and parenting behavior is crucial for the survival and development of the offspring.

Here is an overview of dolphin reproduction and parenting behavior:

Reproduction:

1. **Mating:** Dolphins typically engage in mating activities throughout the year, although there may be seasonal variations depending on the species and location. Mating behaviors include courtship displays, vocalizations, and physical interactions between males and females.

2. **Gestation:** The gestation period for dolphins varies among species but generally ranges from about 10 to 12 months. During pregnancy, female dolphins are known to form close bonds with other females, and they may receive support from pod members.

3. **Calving:** Dolphins give birth to live young, known as calves. Calving can occur throughout the year, although there may be peak calving seasons. The process of giving birth usually takes place in shallow waters.

4. **Mother-Calf Bond:** The bond between a mother dolphin and her calf is exceptionally strong. Mother dolphins are attentive to their calves, providing them with protection, guidance, and nourishment. Calves are born tail-first to reduce the risk of drowning during the birthing process.

Parenting Behavior:

1. **Nursing:** Female dolphins nurse their calves by producing milk from mammary glands located in slits on either side of their genital

region. Calves nurse by latching onto the mother's mammary glands, often swimming alongside the mother for the duration of the nursing period.

2. **Protection and Guidance:** Mother dolphins are highly protective of their calves, especially in the early weeks of life. They guard their offspring against potential threats, and other pod members may also contribute to the protection of the calf. Mothers guide their calves, teaching them essential life skills such as hunting and navigating the environment.

3. **Social Learning:** Dolphin calves learn by observing and mimicking the behaviors of their mothers and other pod members. Social learning is crucial for acquiring skills related to hunting, communication, and navigating their surroundings.

4. **Pod Support:** The extended pod, including relatives and other pod members, plays a role in supporting calf development. Calves may interact with other pod members, including other calves, providing opportunities for socialization and learning.

5. **Weaning:** The weaning process varies among dolphin species but generally occurs over several months to a few years. During this time, the mother gradually reduces nursing, and the calf starts to consume solid food. Weaning is a gradual process, and the bond between mother and calf often remains strong even after nursing has ceased.

6. **Adolescence and Independence:** As calves grow and develop, they become more independent. They may start engaging in social interactions, play, and cooperative behaviors with other pod members. Eventually, they reach a level of maturity where they can actively participate in the activities of the pod.

Dolphin parenting behavior involves a combination of nurturing, protection, and socialization. The strong bonds formed between mothers and calves, as well as the supportive role of the pod, contribute to the successful development and integration of dolphin offspring into the social structure of the pod.

10. Dolphins and Humans

The relationship between dolphins and humans is complex and multifaceted. Dolphins, particularly the bottlenose dolphin, are among the most well-known and charismatic marine animals, and their interactions with humans have been the subject of fascination, scientific study, and various cultural representations.

Here are different aspects of the relationship between dolphins and humans:

1. **Cultural Significance:** Dolphins hold cultural significance in various societies around the world. In many cultures, they are symbols of intelligence, playfulness, and sometimes even spirituality. Dolphins appear in folklore, mythology, and art, often portrayed as positive and benevolent beings.

2. **Tourism and Recreation:** Dolphins are a major attraction in the tourism industry. Many people seek out opportunities to engage in dolphin-watching tours, where they can observe dolphins in their natural habitat. Some places offer the chance to swim with dolphins, although ethical concerns have been raised about the impact of such activities on the animals.

3. **Dolphin-Assisted Therapy:** Some programs claim therapeutic benefits from interactions between dolphins and individuals with physical or psychological challenges. While the therapeutic value of these interactions is debated within the scientific community, dolphin-assisted therapy programs exist in various parts of the world.

4. **Scientific Study:** Dolphins have been subjects of extensive scientific research due to their high level of intelligence, complex social structures, and advanced cognitive abilities. Studies on

dolphin communication, behavior, and cognition have contributed valuable insights into marine mammal biology and intelligence.

5. **Conservation and Education:** The popularity of dolphins has been leveraged for conservation efforts and marine education. Dolphin shows and educational programs in marine parks aim to raise awareness about marine conservation issues and the need to protect ocean environments.

6. **Human-Dolphin Interaction in the Wild:** Dolphins occasionally interact with humans in the wild. There are anecdotal accounts of dolphins approaching boats or swimmers, displaying curiosity or engaging in playful behavior. While such encounters can be positive and memorable, it is essential to respect the animals' space and behave responsibly to avoid disrupting their natural behaviors.

7. **Challenges and Concerns:** Human activities, such as pollution, habitat degradation, overfishing, and accidental entanglement in fishing gear, pose significant threats to dolphins. Dolphins can also be impacted negatively by irresponsible tourism practices, including the disturbance caused by boat traffic and interactions with wild dolphins.

8. **Captivity Controversy:** The practice of keeping dolphins in captivity for entertainment purposes has been a source of controversy. Concerns include the impact on the physical and mental well-being of captive dolphins, ethical considerations regarding their treatment, and the potential for negative consequences on wild populations.

In summary, the relationship between dolphins and humans is multifaceted, encompassing cultural, scientific, recreational, and conservation dimensions. While interactions with dolphins can be positive and enriching, it is crucial to approach such interactions with a deep understanding of and respect for the animals' natural behaviors and needs, as well as their conservation and welfare.

11. Dolphins Conservation Efforts

Dolphin conservation efforts aim to protect these marine mammals and their habitats, address threats to their survival, and promote responsible human interactions.

Here are key aspects of dolphin conservation:

1. **Habitat Protection:**

   - Establishing Marine Protected Areas (MPAs) and sanctuaries to safeguard critical dolphin habitats.

   - Monitoring and regulating coastal development to minimize habitat degradation.

   - Researching and identifying important feeding, breeding, and migratory areas for targeted conservation measures.

2. **Reducing Human Impact:**

   - Implementing and enforcing regulations to reduce water pollution and mitigate the impact of contaminants on dolphins.

   - Addressing issues such as noise pollution, which can interfere with dolphin communication and echolocation.

   - Promoting responsible boating practices to reduce the risk of collisions and disturbance to dolphins.

3. **Fisheries Management:**

   - Implementing sustainable fisheries practices to reduce accidental bycatch of dolphins in fishing gear.

- Developing and promoting dolphin-friendly fishing techniques to minimize negative interactions.

- Collaborating with fishing communities to raise awareness and implement best practices.

4. **Climate Change Mitigation:**

   - Studying the impact of climate change on dolphin habitats and migration patterns.

   - Advocating for global efforts to reduce carbon emissions and mitigate climate change effects on marine ecosystems.

5. **Research and Monitoring:**

   - Conducting scientific research to better understand dolphin behavior, ecology, and population dynamics.

   - Monitoring dolphin populations to assess their health, abundance, and distribution.

   - Using advanced technologies, such as satellite tagging and acoustic monitoring, to gather valuable data.

6. **Community Engagement and Education:**

   - Engaging local communities in dolphin conservation initiatives, emphasizing the importance of healthy marine ecosystems.

   - Conducting educational programs in schools and communities to raise awareness about dolphins and marine conservation.

   - Collaborating with tourism operators to promote responsible and sustainable dolphin-watching practices.

7. **Legislation and Policy Advocacy:**

   - Advocating for and supporting the development of legislation that protects dolphins and their habitats.

- Collaborating with governments, NGOs, and international organizations to establish and enforce conservation policies.

- Participating in international agreements and conventions focused on marine mammal conservation.

8. **Responsible Tourism Practices:**

- Establishing guidelines for responsible dolphin-watching and swimming activities to minimize disturbance.

- Promoting eco-friendly tourism practices that prioritize the well-being of dolphins and their habitats.

- Encouraging the public to choose operators that adhere to ethical standards in dolphin interactions.

9. **Rescue and Rehabilitation:**

- Establishing and supporting marine mammal rescue and rehabilitation centers to respond to stranded or injured dolphins.

- Conducting research on the causes of strandings to inform conservation strategies and mitigate anthropogenic threats.

10. **Collaboration and Partnerships:**

- Collaborating with governmental agencies, non-profit organizations, research institutions, and local communities to create comprehensive conservation strategies.

- Engaging in international partnerships to address transboundary conservation challenges and share best practices.

Dolphin conservation efforts often require a multidisciplinary and collaborative approach, involving scientists, policymakers, communities, and the public to ensure the long-term well-being of these intelligent and charismatic marine mammals.

12. Dolphins Fun Facts

Here are 20 amazing fun facts and statistics about dolphins:

1. **Diverse Species:** There are over 90 species of dolphins, belonging to the family Delphinidae.

2. **Ancient History:** Dolphins have been around for at least 15 million years, based on fossil evidence.

3. **Smart Swimmers:** Dolphins can swim up to 37 mph (60 km/h) and are known for their acrobatic displays, including jumps and flips.

4. **Playful Nature:** Dolphins are highly playful animals and are often seen riding waves and playing with objects like seaweed or bubbles.

5. **Deep Divers:** Some dolphin species can dive to depths of over 1,000 meters (3,280 feet) in search of prey.

6. **Large Brains:** Dolphins have large brains relative to their body size, with a brain-to-body ratio second only to humans among mammals.

7. **Echolocation Range:** Dolphins can use echolocation to detect objects and navigate in waters as far as 820 feet (250 meters) away.

8. **Social Structures:** Dolphins live in social groups called pods, which can range from a few individuals to hundreds.

9. **Individual Whistles:** Dolphins have unique signature whistles, which function like names and are used for individual identification within a pod.

10. **Mating Rituals:** Male dolphins often engage in elaborate courtship displays, including leaping and vocalizations, to attract females.

11. **Birth Underwater:** Dolphins give birth to live calves underwater, and the newborn is immediately brought to the surface for its first breath.

12. **Milk Production:** Female dolphins produce milk with a high-fat content to nourish their calves, aiding in rapid growth.

13. **Longevity:** The average lifespan of a dolphin varies by species but can range from 20 to 60 years.

14. **Global Distribution:** Dolphins are found in oceans and seas around the world, adapting to a wide range of environments.

15. **Racial Recognition:** Dolphins show signs of racial recognition, remembering and associating with dolphins they have encountered before.

16. **Tool Use:** Some dolphins use sponges to protect their rostrums while foraging on the seafloor, showcasing tool-use behavior.

17. **Vocal Repertoire:** Dolphins have a diverse vocal repertoire, including clicks, whistles, and body movements, for communication.

18. **No Sense of Smell:** Dolphins lack a sense of smell and primarily rely on vision and echolocation for navigating and finding food.

19. **Complex Social Bonds:** Dolphins form strong social bonds within their pods and may display cooperative behaviors, such as hunting together.

20. **Incredible Jumpers:** Dolphins are known for their high jumps, and some species, like the common dolphin, can leap as high as 15 feet (4.5 meters) above the water.

These fun facts and statistics highlight the fascinating and diverse nature of dolphins, showcasing their intelligence, adaptability, and unique behaviors.

13. Bottlenose Dolphin

The bottlenose dolphin (Tursiops truncatus) is a charismatic and highly adaptable marine mammal known for its distinctive physical characteristics, intelligence, and social behaviors. These dolphins are found in oceans and seas worldwide, inhabiting a diverse range of environments from coastal areas to offshore waters. Their name is derived from their short and well-defined beak or rostrum, giving the appearance of a bottle-shaped nose.

Physically, bottlenose dolphins have a robust and streamlined body, typically light to dark gray in color on their back, gradually fading to a lighter shade on their belly. A dorsal fin on their back and pectoral fins on either side contribute to their agile and efficient swimming capabilities. The species exhibits sexual dimorphism, with males generally being larger than females.

Bottlenose dolphins are renowned for their intelligence, ranking among the most intelligent animals on Earth. They have a large brain relative to their body size, and their cognitive abilities are evident in problem-solving skills, adaptability, and the capacity to learn from experience. Communication within their social groups, known as pods, is complex and involves a diverse array of clicks, whistles, and body movements. Each individual develops a unique signature whistle, allowing for individual recognition within the pod.

Socially, bottlenose dolphins are highly gregarious and form strong bonds within their pods. Pods can vary in size, and individuals engage in cooperative behaviors such as hunting, herding prey, and providing protection. The social structure is dynamic, and members exhibit empathy and support for one another, particularly during times of vulnerability.

Bottlenose dolphins are opportunistic feeders, consuming a varied diet that includes fish, squid, and crustaceans. They employ different hunting techniques, including herding schools of fish into tight groups and using their tails to stun prey. Their echolocation abilities play a crucial role in navigation, prey detection, and communication, as they emit clicks and interpret the returning echoes.

Due to their adaptability and frequent interactions with humans, bottlenose dolphins hold cultural significance. They are featured in marine parks, where their behaviors are showcased for educational and entertainment purposes. However, conservation concerns exist, as these dolphins face threats such as habitat degradation, pollution, and disturbance from human activities. Conservation efforts aim to address these challenges and ensure the well-being and protection of this iconic marine species.

Here are some ways in which the bottlenose dolphin differs from other dolphins:

1. **Size and Physical Characteristics:**
   - Bottlenose dolphins are of medium to large size, with adults typically ranging from 6 to 13 feet (1.8 to 4 meters) in length. They have a robust body and a prominent, short, and well-defined beak (rostrum), which gives them their characteristic "bottlenose" appearance.
   - Some smaller dolphin species, such as the common dolphin (Delphinus delphis), have a more slender body and a longer beak compared to the bottlenose dolphin.
2. **Dorsal Fin:**
   - The dorsal fin of the bottlenose dolphin is typically tall, curved, and located in the middle of the back. It is a distinguishing feature, and the shape and size can vary among individuals.
   - In contrast, some other dolphin species have different dorsal fin shapes. For example, the orca, or killer whale (Orcinus orca), has a large, triangular dorsal fin.
3. **Geographic Distribution:**
   - Bottlenose dolphins have a global distribution and are found in various environments, including coastal and offshore waters, as well as estuaries and bays. They adapt well to different climates, ranging from temperate to tropical.

- Certain dolphin species, such as the orca, have a wide distribution but may prefer specific regions, including polar seas.

4. **Social Structure:**
   - Bottlenose dolphins are known for their complex and dynamic social structures. They live in groups called pods, and these pods can vary in size from a few individuals to over a hundred.
   - Other dolphin species may have different social structures. For example, some species of river dolphins, like the Amazon River Dolphin, are known to be more solitary.

5. **Intelligence and Interaction with Humans:**
   - Bottlenose dolphins are often featured in marine parks and aquariums due to their high level of intelligence, adaptability to captivity, and ability to learn tricks and behaviors.
   - While other dolphin species, such as the common dolphin, are also intelligent, the bottlenose dolphin has been extensively studied and is perhaps the most well-known and familiar dolphin species to the general public.

6. **Habitat Preferences:**
   - Bottlenose dolphins are highly adaptable and can be found in a wide range of habitats, including coastal, open ocean, and estuarine environments.
   - Some species, like the spinner dolphin (Stenella longirostris), are more often associated with offshore waters and are known for their acrobatic spinning behavior.

14. Killer Whale or Orca

The killer whale, or orca (Orcinus orca), is one of the most iconic and widely recognized marine mammals. Known for its distinctive black and white coloration and large dorsal fin, the killer whale is a member of the dolphin family (Delphinidae). Here are some key features that characterize the killer whale:

Physical Characteristics: Killer whales are easily distinguishable by their striking black and white color pattern. They have a robust body, a tall and straight dorsal fin (which can reach up to 6 feet or 1.8 meters in height in males), and white patches near their eyes and on their belly. The size and shape of the white markings vary among individuals and populations.

Global Distribution: Killer whales have a global distribution and are found in oceans from the Arctic to the Antarctic. They inhabit both cold and warm waters, including coastal and offshore environments. Different populations of killer whales may display variations in diet, behavior, and vocalizations.

Diet and Hunting Strategies: Killer whales are apex predators and exhibit diverse feeding habits. While some populations primarily feed on fish, others are known to hunt marine mammals, including seals, sea lions, and even other whale species. Certain killer whale populations have developed unique hunting strategies, such as intentional beaching to capture seals.

Social Structure: Killer whales live in highly social groups known as pods. These pods are matriarchal, with the eldest female leading the group. Family bonds are strong within pods, and members engage in cooperative behaviors such as hunting and caring for calves. Pods can vary in size and structure, with some consisting of only a few individuals, while others comprise dozens.

Communication and Vocalizations: Killer whales are known for their complex communication system, which involves a variety of vocalizations such as clicks, whistles, and pulsed calls. Each pod has its distinct set of vocalizations, contributing to the identification and communication within the group. Killer whales also use echolocation for navigation and locating prey.

Cultural Traits: Some killer whale populations exhibit cultural traits, including unique hunting techniques and vocalizations that are passed down from generation to generation. This cultural transmission highlights the adaptability and intelligence of these marine mammals.

Conservation Status: Killer whales face various threats, including pollution, habitat degradation, and the depletion of prey species. While they are not currently listed as a globally endangered species, certain populations, such as the Southern Resident killer whales in the Pacific Northwest, are considered at risk due to factors like declining salmon populations and disturbances from boat traffic.

The killer whale's intelligence, adaptability, and charismatic presence have contributed to its popularity in marine parks and cultural representations. However, conservation efforts are crucial to ensure the well-being and protection of these remarkable marine mammals in the wild.

15. Common Dolphin

The term "common dolphin" actually refers to two distinct species of dolphins: the short-beaked common dolphin (Delphinus delphis) and the long-beaked common dolphin (Delphinus capensis). Both species share some general characteristics that categorize them as common dolphins.

Physical Characteristics: Common dolphins are known for their sleek and streamlined bodies, which are well-adapted for swift and agile swimming. As their names suggest, the short-beaked common dolphin has a shorter and more rounded beak, while the long-beaked common dolphin has a more elongated snout. They both exhibit a distinctive hourglass pattern on their sides, featuring yellow-tan patches on a grayish background. Their dorsal fins are sharply curved, and they are highly capable swimmers, often engaging in energetic behaviors like leaping and riding the bow waves created by ships.

Size and Distribution: Common dolphins are of medium size compared to other dolphin species. They typically range from 6 to 8 feet (1.8 to 2.4 meters) in length, with some variation between the two species. They are found in oceans around the world, occupying both warm and temperate waters. The short-beaked common dolphin is more widely distributed and can be found in both offshore and coastal environments, while the long-beaked common dolphin tends to prefer more offshore habitats.

Social Structure and Behavior: Common dolphins are highly social animals and are often observed in groups called pods. These pods can vary in size, ranging from a few individuals to several hundred. Within these pods, common dolphins engage in various social behaviors, including hunting, communication, and playful activities. They are known for their acrobatic displays, which may involve leaping, somersaulting, and riding the wakes of boats.

Feeding Habits: Common dolphins are opportunistic feeders with a diet that includes a variety of fish and squid. They are known to work cooperatively when hunting, herding schools of fish into tight groups before taking turns to feed. This cooperative hunting behavior allows them to efficiently locate and capture prey.

Vocalizations: Like other dolphin species, common dolphins are highly vocal and use a diverse range of clicks, whistles, and body movements for communication. They have signature whistles that are thought to be used for individual recognition within the pod.

Conservation Status: While common dolphins are not currently considered globally endangered, certain populations may face threats from human activities such as bycatch in fishing gear, pollution, and habitat degradation. Conservation efforts aim to address these challenges and protect the well-being of common dolphin populations.

In summary, common dolphins are characterized by their distinctive appearance, social nature, and playful behavior. Their adaptability to various environments and their interactions with humans make them a subject of interest in marine biology and conservation efforts.

16. Spinner Dolphin

Spinner dolphins (genus Stenella) are a group of small to medium-sized dolphins known for their acrobatic displays, particularly their spinning leaps and jumps. There are several species of spinner dolphins, including the common spinner dolphin (Stenella longirostris), which is the most widely recognized. Here are some key characteristics and features of spinner dolphins:

Physical Characteristics: Spinner dolphins have a slender and streamlined body, and their name is derived from their remarkable spinning behavior. They are easily identifiable by a distinctive three-part color pattern. The dorsal (upper) side is typically dark gray, the flanks (sides) have a light gray or tan color, and the ventral (underside) region is white or light gray. They also have a long, slender beak and a dark eye patch.

Spinner Behavior: One of the most notable behaviors of spinner dolphins is their aerial displays. These dolphins are known for leaping out of the water and making multiple spins or somersaults before re-entering the water. This behavior is thought to serve various purposes, including communication, play, and possibly to dislodge parasites. Spinner dolphins are often observed engaging in these acrobatic displays during the day, particularly in the morning and late afternoon.

Social Structure and Pods: Spinner dolphins are highly social animals and are typically found in groups or pods. These pods can vary in size but are often composed of several hundred individuals. They exhibit strong social bonds within the pod and engage in cooperative behaviors, including hunting and protection. Spinner dolphins are known for their tight-knit social structure, and they may even form larger aggregations with other dolphin species.

Feeding Habits: Spinner dolphins are nocturnal feeders, meaning they hunt for food during the night. They primarily feed on small fish, squid, and other small marine organisms. During their nighttime foraging activities, they often dive to significant depths to locate prey.

Global Distribution: Spinner dolphins have a wide distribution and can be found in tropical and subtropical waters around the world. They inhabit offshore and pelagic environments, often occurring near islands and continental shelves.

Conservation Status: While spinner dolphins are not considered globally endangered, certain populations may face localized threats, including bycatch in fishing gear, disturbance from boat traffic, and habitat degradation. Conservation efforts aim to address these challenges and ensure the protection of spinner dolphin populations.

In summary, spinner dolphins are known for their playful and acrobatic behavior, captivating onlookers with their spinning leaps. Their social nature and widespread distribution make them an interesting subject of study and observation for marine biologists and enthusiasts alike.

17. Risso's Dolphin

Risso's dolphin (Grampus griseus) is a distinctive and medium to large-sized species of dolphin known for its unique appearance and behavior.

Here are some key features and characteristics of Risso's dolphin:

Physical Characteristics: Risso's dolphins have a robust and stocky body with a blunt head and no discernible beak. Their most distinguishing feature is their unusual coloration. When born, Risso's dolphins are dark gray to black, but as they age, their bodies accumulate scars and marks from social interactions and interactions with prey, resulting in a lighter appearance. Older individuals can have almost entirely white bodies, giving them a striking and mottled appearance. These markings often include linear scars caused by the teeth of other Risso's dolphins during social interactions.

Size and Distribution: Adult Risso's dolphins typically measure between 8 to 12 feet (2.4 to 3.7 meters) in length, with males generally larger than females. They are found in temperate and tropical waters worldwide, inhabiting both offshore and deep oceanic environments. Risso's dolphins are often associated with deeper waters, where they can be observed in groups or pods.

Social Structure and Behavior: Risso's dolphins are social animals and are often found in groups that can range from a few individuals to larger pods of several dozen. They are known for their acrobatic displays, including breaching, tail-slapping, and fluke-slapping. Risso's dolphins are vocal communicators, using clicks and whistles for social interactions and navigation. They are also known to bow-ride, where they swim in the wake of boats.

Feeding Habits: Risso's dolphins have a diverse diet that includes squid, octopus, and various fish species. They are skilled hunters and have been observed cooperating in groups to locate and catch prey. Their teeth are relatively few and peg-like, adapted for grasping and holding onto slippery prey such as squid.

Conservation Status: The conservation status of Risso's dolphins is currently listed as "Data Deficient" by the International Union for Conservation of Nature (IUCN). This classification reflects a lack of comprehensive data on population size, distribution, and threats. Risso's dolphins are vulnerable to entanglement in fishing gear, particularly in areas where they overlap with fisheries.

In summary, Risso's dolphins are characterized by their distinctive appearance, social behavior, and the accumulation of markings on their bodies over time. While they are not as well-studied as some other dolphin species, ongoing research efforts aim to better understand their ecology, population dynamics, and conservation needs.

18. Pacific White-Sided Dolphin

The Pacific white-sided dolphin (Lagenorhynchus obliquidens) is a charismatic and highly social marine mammal found in the North Pacific Ocean. Here are key features and characteristics of the Pacific white-sided dolphin:

Physical Characteristics: Pacific white-sided dolphins have a robust and streamlined body with a short, beakless snout. Their distinctive coloration includes a dark gray to black back, a white belly, and light gray or off-white patches on their sides. This striking pattern creates a vivid contrast, making them easily recognizable. They have a tall, falcate dorsal fin, and their flippers are also prominently marked with contrasting colors.

Size and Distribution: Adult Pacific white-sided dolphins typically measure between 6 to 8 feet (1.8 to 2.4 meters) in length, with males generally larger than females. They inhabit the cool temperate and subarctic waters of the North Pacific Ocean. Their range extends from the western coast of North America, including California and Alaska, to the eastern coast of Asia, including Japan.

Social Structure and Behavior: Pacific white-sided dolphins are known for their gregarious and social nature. They often travel in large, dynamic groups called pods, which can consist of several dozen to hundreds of individuals. These pods are known for their acrobatic displays, including leaps, spins, and somersaults. Pacific white-sided dolphins are also enthusiastic bow-riders, surfing the bow waves created by boats.

Feeding Habits: These dolphins are opportunistic feeders with a diverse diet that includes fish, squid, and small crustaceans. They are skilled hunters and may work together to herd schools of fish for efficient feeding. Their ability to swim swiftly and perform agile maneuvers aids in capturing prey.

Vocalizations: Pacific white-sided dolphins use a variety of vocalizations, including whistles, clicks, and pulsed sounds, for communication within their pods. These vocalizations play a crucial role in maintaining social bonds, coordinating group movements, and possibly locating prey.

Conservation Status: The conservation status of Pacific white-sided dolphins is considered to be of "Least Concern" by the International Union for Conservation of Nature (IUCN). While they are not currently facing significant threats, these dolphins may be affected by human activities such as habitat degradation, pollution, and disturbance from boat traffic. Ongoing monitoring and conservation efforts are essential to ensure their well-being in the wild.

In summary, the Pacific white-sided dolphin is known for its striking appearance, social behavior, and acrobatic displays. Its wide distribution across the North Pacific Ocean makes it a captivating species for marine enthusiasts and researchers studying the diverse marine ecosystems of the region.

19. Dusky Dolphin

The dusky dolphin (Lagenorhynchus obscurus) is a medium-sized species of dolphin known for its distinctive coloration, acrobatic behavior, and widespread distribution in cool and temperate waters around the world. Here are key features and characteristics of the dusky dolphin:

Physical Characteristics: Dusky dolphins have a sleek and robust body with a short beak and a rounded melon. Their coloration is notable for a distinct dark gray to black back, a light grayish-tan lateral area, and a white belly. This creates a sharp and visually striking contrast along their body. They have a falcate dorsal fin and long flippers, contributing to their agile swimming capabilities.

Size and Distribution: Adult dusky dolphins typically measure between 5.5 to 6.5 feet (1.7 to 2 meters) in length, with males generally larger than females. They are found in cool and temperate waters of the Southern Hemisphere, including the southern coasts of South America, Africa, Australia, and New Zealand. Dusky dolphins are also known to inhabit offshore waters and oceanic islands.

Social Structure and Behavior: Dusky dolphins are highly social animals and are often encountered in large groups or pods that can consist of dozens to hundreds of individuals. These pods exhibit coordinated and playful behaviors, with dusky dolphins being particularly known for their acrobatic displays. They are skilled swimmers and frequently engage in leaps, flips, and spins, creating a spectacle for observers. Dusky dolphins are also known for their interactions with boats, often riding the bow waves and wake created by vessels.

Feeding Habits: Dusky dolphins are opportunistic feeders with a diet that includes various species of fish and squid. They are known for their cooperative hunting techniques, using the power of their pod to corral and concentrate schools of fish for efficient feeding. Their agility and speed play a crucial role in capturing prey.

Vocalizations: Dusky dolphins communicate using a diverse array of vocalizations, including clicks, whistles, and burst-pulse sounds. These vocalizations serve purposes such as social bonding, coordinating group movements, and potentially locating prey.

Conservation Status: The conservation status of dusky dolphins is generally considered to be of "Least Concern" by the International Union for Conservation of Nature (IUCN). However, they may face localized threats such as bycatch in fishing gear, habitat degradation, and disturbance from boat traffic. Conservation efforts aim to mitigate these potential threats and protect dusky dolphin populations.

In summary, the dusky dolphin is characterized by its striking coloration, social behavior, and acrobatic displays. Its presence in the cool waters of the Southern Hemisphere makes it a captivating species for marine enthusiasts and researchers studying marine ecosystems in these regions.

20. Pantropical Spotted Dolphin

The pantropical spotted dolphin (Stenella attenuata) is a species of dolphin known for its distinctive spotted coloration and widespread distribution in warm and tropical waters around the world. Here are key features and characteristics of the pantropical spotted dolphin:

Physical Characteristics: Pantropical spotted dolphins have a sleek and slender body with a relatively long, beak-like snout. Their most recognizable feature is the complex spotted pattern on their body, which consists of dark spots or flecks on a light gray or light tan background. The spots are more concentrated on the dorsal (upper) side and become less distinct on the ventral (underside) side. They have a tall, falcate dorsal fin, and their flippers are also prominently marked with spots.

Size and Distribution: Adult pantropical spotted dolphins typically measure between 6 to 7 feet (1.8 to 2.1 meters) in length. They are found in tropical and subtropical waters of the world, with a distribution that spans the Pacific, Atlantic, and Indian Oceans. Their range includes regions such as the eastern Pacific, western Atlantic, and the Indo-Pacific.

Social Structure and Behavior: Pantropical spotted dolphins are highly social animals and are often encountered in large groups or pods that can consist of dozens to hundreds of individuals. These pods are known for their playful and acrobatic behaviors, including leaps, spins, and bow-riding. They are often observed riding the bow waves created by boats, exhibiting a high level of curiosity and interaction with vessels.

Feeding Habits: These dolphins are opportunistic feeders with a diet that includes various species of fish and squid. They may use coordinated hunting strategies, such as herding schools of fish to facilitate efficient feeding. Their agility and speed are important for capturing prey.

Vocalizations: Pantropical spotted dolphins communicate using a variety of vocalizations, including whistles, clicks, and burst-pulse sounds. These vocalizations serve important functions within the pod, including maintaining social bonds, coordinating movements, and potentially locating prey.

Conservation Status: The conservation status of pantropical spotted dolphins is generally considered to be of "Least Concern" by the International Union for Conservation of Nature (IUCN). While they are not currently facing significant threats on a global scale, localized populations may be vulnerable to threats such as bycatch in fishing gear, habitat degradation, and disturbances from human activities.

In summary, the pantropical spotted dolphin is characterized by its distinctive spotted pattern, social behavior, and acrobatic displays. Its widespread distribution in warm and tropical waters makes it a fascinating species for marine enthusiasts and researchers studying marine ecosystems across the globe.

21. Striped Dolphin

The striped dolphin (Stenella coeruleoalba) is a species of dolphin known for its sleek appearance and striking coloration. Here are key features and characteristics of the striped dolphin:

Physical Characteristics: The striped dolphin has a slender and streamlined body with a long, beak-like snout. Its most distinctive feature is the prominent color pattern, which consists of dark blue or black stripes along the length of its body. These stripes run from the eye to the flipper and along the sides, creating a visually striking contrast with the light gray or white color of the rest of the body. The dorsal fin is falcate and the flippers are long and slender.

Size and Distribution: Adult striped dolphins typically measure between 6 to 8 feet (1.8 to 2.5 meters) in length. They are found in warm and temperate waters worldwide, with a distribution that includes the Atlantic and Pacific Oceans, as well as the Mediterranean Sea. Striped dolphins are often associated with offshore and deep-sea environments.

Social Structure and Behavior: Striped dolphins are highly social animals and are often encountered in large groups or pods that can consist of dozens to hundreds of individuals. These pods are known for their coordinated swimming, playful behaviors, and acrobatic displays, including leaping and riding bow waves. Striped dolphins are also known to engage in porpoising, a behavior where they leap out of the water in a series of rapid jumps.

Feeding Habits: Striped dolphins are opportunistic feeders with a diet that includes various species of fish and squid. They are known to hunt cooperatively, herding schools of fish for efficient feeding. Their slender body and agility play a crucial role in capturing prey.

Vocalizations: Striped dolphins communicate using a diverse range of vocalizations, including clicks, whistles, and burst-pulse sounds. These vocalizations serve important functions within the pod, including maintaining social bonds, coordinating movements, and potentially locating prey.

Conservation Status: The conservation status of striped dolphins is generally considered to be of "Least Concern" by the International Union for Conservation of Nature (IUCN). While they are not facing significant global threats, certain populations may be vulnerable to localized threats such as bycatch in fishing gear, habitat degradation, and disturbances from human activities.

In summary, the striped dolphin is characterized by its sleek body, distinctive coloration, and social behavior. Its presence in warm and temperate seas makes it a captivating species for marine enthusiasts and researchers studying the diverse ecosystems of these regions.

22. Amazon River Dolphin

The Amazon River dolphin, scientifically known as Inia geoffrensis, is a unique and fascinating species of freshwater dolphin found in the Amazon River Basin of South America. Here are key features and characteristics of the Amazon River dolphin:

Physical Characteristics: The Amazon River dolphin displays a distinctive appearance, featuring a robust and flexible body with a long snout. It lacks a pronounced dorsal fin, and its flippers are broad and paddle-shaped. What truly sets the Amazon River dolphin apart is its variable coloration. Individuals can range from light pink to gray or brown, depending on factors such as age, water clarity, and overall health. Older individuals often have more noticeable color variations.

Habitat and Distribution: Amazon River dolphins primarily inhabit the slow-moving, murky waters of the Amazon River and its tributaries, including flooded forests and lakes. They are well-adapted to navigate through complex and dynamic river environments, utilizing echolocation to navigate and locate prey in low-visibility conditions.

Social Structure and Behavior: These dolphins are known for their solitary and social behaviors. While they are often observed alone or in small groups, they can form larger aggregations in areas with abundant food resources. Amazon River dolphins are known to engage in cooperative behaviors, such as hunting in groups and working together to catch fish. Their social structure and behaviors are adapted to the challenges of living in complex riverine ecosystems.

Feeding Habits: Amazon River dolphins primarily feed on various fish species found in their habitat. They use echolocation to detect prey, emitting sounds that bounce off objects in the water, helping them navigate and locate food. The dolphins are opportunistic feeders, adjusting their feeding strategies based on the availability of prey in different parts of the river.

Cultural Significance: Amazon River dolphins hold cultural significance for local communities in the Amazon Basin. In some indigenous beliefs, these dolphins are considered sacred and possess mystical qualities. However, they face threats from human activities, including habitat degradation, pollution, and accidental entanglement in fishing gear.

Conservation Status: The conservation status of Amazon River dolphins varies across their range, but they face threats due to habitat loss, pollution, and fisheries interactions. The International Union for Conservation of Nature (IUCN) lists them as a species of "Least Concern," but regional populations may be at greater risk, particularly in areas with increased human impact.

In summary, the Amazon River dolphin is an iconic and ecologically important species, intricately connected to the rich and diverse ecosystems of the Amazon River Basin. Conservation efforts aim to address threats and preserve the unique cultural and ecological role of these dolphins in the region.

23. Irrawaddy Dolphin

The Irrawaddy dolphin (Orcaella brevirostris) is a distinctive and unique species of dolphin found in rivers, estuaries, and coastal areas across Southeast and South Asia. Here are key features and characteristics of the Irrawaddy dolphin:

Physical Characteristics: Irrawaddy dolphins have a robust and bulbous head with a short and rounded beak, lacking the long snout typical of many other dolphin species. Their melon, the rounded area of their forehead, is particularly prominent. The dorsal fin is small and triangular, and the flippers are broad and paddle-shaped. The coloration of Irrawaddy dolphins varies, with individuals ranging from light gray to dark slate gray. They lack the distinct color patterns seen in some other dolphin species.

Habitat and Distribution: Irrawaddy dolphins are primarily found in freshwater habitats, including rivers, estuaries, and coastal areas. They inhabit a range that extends from the Bay of Bengal and Southeast Asia to northern Australia and the Philippines. These dolphins are well-adapted to both freshwater and marine environments and have been observed in riverine systems such as the Irrawaddy River in Myanmar and the Mekong River in Southeast Asia.

Social Structure and Behavior: Irrawaddy dolphins are known for their social behavior, often forming small groups or pods. These pods can consist of a few individuals to larger groups, and they are observed engaging in cooperative behaviors such as hunting and socializing. Irrawaddy dolphins are known to exhibit a behavior called "spyhopping," where they raise their heads vertically out of the water to observe their surroundings.

Feeding Habits: These dolphins primarily feed on a variety of fish and invertebrates found in their habitat. They use echolocation, emitting sounds that bounce off objects in the water, to locate prey. Irrawaddy dolphins may also use their flippers to herd schools of fish and disorient them before feeding.

Conservation Status: The conservation status of Irrawaddy dolphins varies across their range. Some populations are considered vulnerable or endangered due to threats such as habitat loss, entanglement in fishing gear, and pollution. Conservation efforts focus on protecting their habitats, mitigating human impacts, and ensuring sustainable practices to safeguard the future of these unique dolphins.

Cultural Significance: Irrawaddy dolphins hold cultural significance in some communities, and they are often associated with folklore and local traditions. In certain regions, these dolphins are considered sacred or bringers of good fortune.

In summary, the Irrawaddy dolphin is a remarkable species adapted to both freshwater and marine environments, playing a crucial role in the ecosystems of rivers and estuaries in Southeast and South Asia. Conservation efforts are vital to address the threats they face and ensure the continued existence of these charismatic dolphins.

24. Indo-Pacific Humpback Dolphin

The Indo-Pacific humpback dolphin (Sousa chinensis) is a distinct and visually striking species of dolphin found in the coastal waters of the Indian and Western Pacific Oceans. Here are key features and characteristics of the Indo-Pacific humpback dolphin:

Physical Characteristics: The Indo-Pacific humpback dolphin is easily recognizable by its unique appearance. Adults typically have a pink to grayish-pink coloration, and their bodies may have irregular spots, patches, or speckling. One of the most distinctive features is the hump that is evident just below the dorsal fin. The dorsal fin itself is relatively small and triangular. Indo-Pacific humpback dolphins have a long beak and a stocky body.

Habitat and Distribution: These dolphins inhabit a variety of coastal environments, including estuaries, bays, and shallow coastal waters. Their range extends from the eastern coast of Africa across the Indian Ocean to the western Pacific, including areas around Southeast Asia, northern Australia, and parts of southern China. They are known to prefer shallow coastal areas with muddy or sandy substrates.

Social Structure and Behavior: Indo-Pacific humpback dolphins are social animals and are often observed in small groups or pods, typically consisting of a few individuals to around 20. They are known for their acrobatic behaviors, including leaping, tail-slapping, and bow-riding. These dolphins are also skilled hunters, using their intelligence and cooperative strategies to catch fish and other prey.

Feeding Habits: The diet of Indo-Pacific humpback dolphins primarily consists of a variety of fish and invertebrates found in their coastal habitats. They use echolocation to locate and catch prey, emitting sounds that bounce off objects in the water, providing them with a detailed understanding of their environment.

Conservation Status: The conservation status of Indo-Pacific humpback dolphins varies across their range. Some populations face threats such as habitat degradation, fisheries interactions, and coastal development. Certain subpopulations are classified as vulnerable or endangered. Conservation efforts focus on understanding their distribution, mitigating human impacts, and implementing measures to protect their habitats.

Cultural Significance: Indo-Pacific humpback dolphins hold cultural significance in some communities, and they are often featured in local folklore and traditions. In some areas, they are considered sacred or are associated with positive symbolism.

In summary, the Indo-Pacific humpback dolphin is a captivating species with its distinctive coloration and hump. Its coastal habitat and social behaviors make it an interesting subject for study and conservation efforts aimed at safeguarding their populations in the diverse marine environments they inhabit.

:

25. Fraser's Dolphin

Fraser's dolphin (Lagenodelphis hosei) is a species of marine dolphin known for its sleek appearance, distinctive coloration, and widespread distribution in tropical and subtropical waters. Here are key features and characteristics of Fraser's dolphin:

Physical Characteristics: Fraser's dolphins have a slender and streamlined body with a long beak, and they lack a pronounced rostrum. Their dorsal fin is tall and falcate, curving backward, and the flippers are long and pointed. The most striking feature is their unique color pattern, which includes a dark blue to black patch that extends from the beak to the melon (forehead), contrasting with a light gray or pinkish body. The patch creates a noticeable hourglass shape on their sides, distinguishing them from other dolphin species.

Size and Distribution: Adult Fraser's dolphins typically measure between 6.6 to 8.2 feet (2 to 2.5 meters) in length. They are found in tropical and subtropical waters across the world, with a distribution that includes the Atlantic, Pacific, and Indian Oceans. Fraser's dolphins are often associated with deep offshore habitats, and they are known to inhabit both pelagic and continental slope environments.

Social Structure and Behavior: Fraser's dolphins are social animals and are often encountered in large groups or pods that can consist of several hundred individuals. These pods exhibit coordinated swimming and are known for their acrobatic behaviors, including leaps, spins, and porpoising (rapid jumping in and out of the water). Fraser's dolphins are particularly active at the surface, making them a captivating species to observe.

Feeding Habits: The diet of Fraser's dolphins primarily consists of small fish and squid. They are skilled hunters, using their echolocation abilities to locate and capture prey in deep offshore waters. These dolphins are known to engage in cooperative hunting, with individuals working together to corral and capture schools of fish.

Vocalizations: Fraser's dolphins communicate using a variety of vocalizations, including clicks and whistles. These vocalizations play a crucial role in maintaining social bonds within the pod and coordinating group movements during activities such as hunting.

Conservation Status: The conservation status of Fraser's dolphins is generally considered to be of "Least Concern" by the International Union for Conservation of Nature (IUCN). While they are not facing significant global threats, they may be vulnerable to certain localized impacts such as fisheries interactions, habitat degradation, and noise pollution.

In summary, Fraser's dolphins are characterized by their striking coloration, social behavior, and acrobatic displays. Their wide distribution in offshore tropical and subtropical waters makes them a fascinating subject for researchers studying marine ecosystems in these regions.

26. Hector's Dolphin

Hector's dolphin (Cephalorhynchus hectori) is a small and distinctive species of dolphin endemic to the coastal waters of New Zealand. Named after Sir James Hector, a 19th-century scientist, these dolphins are known for their unique appearance and limited distribution. Here are key features and characteristics of Hector's dolphin:

Physical Characteristics: Hector's dolphins are one of the smallest dolphin species, with adults typically measuring around 4 feet (1.2 meters) in length. They have a distinctive rounded dorsal fin and a relatively short and blunt beak. Their coloration is notable, featuring a striking black dorsal fin, a light gray or white ventral side, and a distinctive hourglass-shaped marking on their sides. This marking varies in intensity among individuals and serves as a key identifying feature.

Habitat and Distribution: Hector's dolphins are found in the coastal waters of New Zealand, particularly around the South Island and the West Coast of the North Island. They inhabit shallow coastal areas, including harbors, bays, and estuaries. Within their limited range, they have adapted to a variety of coastal habitats.

Social Structure and Behavior: Hector's dolphins are social animals often found in small groups or pods. These pods typically consist of a few individuals to around a dozen dolphins. They are known for their playful and acrobatic behaviors, including leaping, riding waves, and engaging in synchronized swimming. Their social structure and behavior make them a popular species for wildlife watching in New Zealand.

Feeding Habits: The diet of Hector's dolphins primarily consists of small fish and invertebrates, including various species of fish, squid, and crustaceans. They use echolocation to locate and capture prey in the often turbid coastal waters they inhabit.

Conservation Status: Hector's dolphins are classified as endangered by the International Union for Conservation of Nature (IUCN). They face several threats, including habitat degradation, entanglement in fishing gear, and disturbance from human activities. Specific subpopulations, such as the Maui dolphin, are critically endangered, with very small numbers remaining. Conservation efforts focus on mitigating these threats, implementing conservation measures, and raising awareness to protect these unique dolphins.

Conservation Efforts: Various conservation initiatives are underway to protect Hector's dolphins. These include establishing marine reserves, implementing fishing restrictions in critical habitats, and promoting sustainable tourism practices. Efforts are also directed at reducing bycatch in fishing gear and addressing other human-induced threats to their survival.

In summary, Hector's dolphin is a charismatic and endangered species that plays a vital role in the coastal ecosystems of New Zealand. Conservation efforts are crucial to ensure the survival and well-being of these unique dolphins in their limited and vulnerable habitats.

27. Commerson's Dolphin

Commerson's dolphin (Cephalorhynchus commersonii), also known as the skunk dolphin or panda dolphin, is a small and distinctive species of dolphin found in cold and sub-Antarctic waters. Here are key features and characteristics of Commerson's dolphin:

Physical Characteristics: Commerson's dolphins are easily recognizable by their striking black-and-white coloration, which resembles that of a panda. They have a robust and rounded body with a short beak, and their dorsal fin is small and triangular. The black coloration covers the head, back, and flippers, while the rest of the body, including the belly and tail, is white. The clear contrast between black and white makes them one of the most visually distinctive dolphin species.

Size and Distribution: Adult Commerson's dolphins typically measure between 3 to 4 feet (0.9 to 1.2 meters) in length. They are found in cold, sub-Antarctic waters, including the southern coasts of South America, the Kerguelen Islands, and the sub-Antarctic islands in the Indian and Pacific Oceans. They prefer coastal habitats, including bays, estuaries, and nearshore areas.

Social Structure and Behavior: Commerson's dolphins are social animals and are often observed in small groups or pods. These pods can consist of a few individuals to around 20 dolphins. They are known for their playful and acrobatic behaviors, including leaping, porpoising, and riding bow waves created by boats. Commerson's dolphins are curious and may approach vessels, making them a popular species for wildlife observation.

Feeding Habits: The diet of Commerson's dolphins primarily consists of small fish and invertebrates found in their coastal habitats. They use echolocation to locate and capture prey, emitting sounds that bounce off objects in the water to create a mental map of their surroundings.

Conservation Status: Commerson's dolphins are generally considered to be of "Least Concern" by the International Union for Conservation of Nature (IUCN) due to their relatively stable population and widespread distribution. However, certain populations may face localized threats, such as habitat degradation, pollution, and accidental entanglement in fishing gear.

Conservation Efforts: While overall conservation status is relatively favorable, ongoing monitoring and research are essential to understand and mitigate potential threats to Commerson's dolphins. Conservation efforts may include measures to protect their coastal habitats, regulate human activities in their range, and address specific threats that could impact their well-being.

In summary, Commerson's dolphin is a visually striking and socially active species found in cold, coastal waters. Their distinctive black-and-white coloration and playful behaviors make them a captivating species for marine enthusiasts and researchers studying the marine ecosystems of sub-Antarctic regions.

28. Pigmy Killer Whale

The pygmy killer whale (Feresa attenuata) is a relatively small and elusive species of toothed whale belonging to the oceanic dolphin family. Here are key features and characteristics of the pygmy killer whale:

Physical Characteristics: Pygmy killer whales have a sleek and robust body with a rounded head and a short, barely noticeable beak. They have a distinctive coloration, featuring a dark gray to black body with a lighter gray or white anchor-shaped patch on their chest. This patch extends up to the throat and creates a unique and recognizable marking. Their dorsal fin is curved and falcate, and they have a pair of small, pointed flippers. Adults typically measure around 6 to 8 feet (1.8 to 2.4 meters) in length.

Habitat and Distribution: Pygmy killer whales are found in warm tropical and subtropical waters around the world. They inhabit deep offshore waters, making them challenging to study and observe. While they prefer deep-sea environments, they have been occasionally sighted near continental shelves and oceanic islands.

Social Structure and Behavior: Pygmy killer whales are known for their social nature and are often observed in groups or pods that can range from a few individuals to over a hundred. These pods are tightly knit, and individuals within a pod exhibit coordinated swimming and behaviors. They are skilled and powerful swimmers, known for their rapid acceleration and agility.

Feeding Habits: The diet of pygmy killer whales primarily consists of fish and squid. They are known to be opportunistic feeders, hunting in deep-sea environments where they can target a variety of prey species. The exact details of their feeding behavior are not well-documented due to the challenges of studying them in their offshore habitats.

Vocalizations: Pygmy killer whales produce a range of vocalizations, including whistles and clicks. These vocalizations are believed to play a role in communication within the pod, coordinating group movements, and potentially locating prey.

Conservation Status: The conservation status of pygmy killer whales is not well-documented, and their populations are considered to be data-deficient by the International Union for Conservation of Nature (IUCN). Due to their offshore habitat and elusive nature, assessing population trends and potential threats remains challenging.

In summary, the pygmy killer whale is a fascinating species known for its distinctive coloration and social behavior. Their preference for deep offshore waters makes them a species that is less frequently encountered, and ongoing research is necessary to better understand their ecology and conservation needs.

29. False Killer Whale

The false killer whale (Pseudorca crassidens) is a large and powerful species of dolphin that shares some physical characteristics with the true killer whale (orca), hence its name. Here are key features and characteristics of the false killer whale:

Physical Characteristics: False killer whales have a robust and streamlined body with a prominent, rounded melon on their forehead. Their coloration is generally dark, ranging from dark gray to black, and they often have a light gray or white patch on their ventral side, extending from the throat to the belly. One distinctive feature is their long, slender, and slightly curved dorsal fin, which can reach lengths of over two meters (six feet). Their flippers are also long and pointed.

Size and Distribution: Adult false killer whales are among the larger dolphin species, with males typically larger than females. They can reach lengths of up to 20 feet (6 meters) or more. False killer whales are found in warm and temperate oceanic waters around the world, including tropical and subtropical regions. They are known to inhabit both offshore and deep-sea environments.

Social Structure and Behavior: False killer whales are highly social animals and are often observed in large groups called pods. These pods can consist of several dozen to over a hundred individuals. They are known for their acrobatic behavior, including breaching, leaping, and riding the bow waves created by boats. False killer whales are also known to engage in cooperative hunting, working together to capture prey, which can include fish and squid.

Feeding Habits: False killer whales are opportunistic predators with a diverse diet. They are known to hunt and feed on various fish species, squid, and, on occasion, other marine mammals. They are powerful swimmers and can cover large distances in search of prey. Their cooperative hunting strategies make them effective hunters.

Vocalizations: False killer whales are known for their complex vocalizations, which include a variety of whistles, clicks, and pulsed sounds. These vocalizations are believed to play a crucial role in communication within the pod, coordinating group movements, and possibly locating prey.

Conservation Status: The conservation status of false killer whales varies among populations. Some populations are considered vulnerable due to threats such as fisheries interactions, habitat degradation, and pollution. Conservation efforts focus on understanding and mitigating these threats, as well as promoting sustainable practices to protect these marine mammals.

In summary, the false killer whale is a remarkable species known for its social behavior, distinctive appearance, and powerful swimming abilities. While they share some physical characteristics with true killer whales, they are a distinct species with their own ecological roles and conservation needs.

30. Narwhal

The narwhal (Monodon monoceros) is a fascinating and unique species of toothed whale known for its long, spiral tusk that can reach lengths of up to 10 feet (3 meters). Here are key features and characteristics of the narwhal:

Physical Characteristics: The most distinctive feature of the narwhal is its long, spiral tusk, which is actually an elongated tooth. While the purpose of the tusk is not entirely understood, it is believed to play a role in communication, sensory perception, and possibly in breaking through sea ice. Male narwhals typically have a single tusk, while females may have a smaller tusk or none at all. Narwhals also have a mottled gray or brownish coloration that helps them blend in with their Arctic surroundings.

Habitat and Distribution: Narwhals inhabit Arctic and subarctic waters, with their range extending from the Canadian Arctic to the Russian Arctic. They are adapted to life in icy environments and are known to travel great distances in their seasonal migrations. Narwhals are well-suited for life in cold waters, with a thick layer of blubber to provide insulation.

Social Structure and Behavior: Narwhals are social animals that often travel in groups called pods. These pods can vary in size, ranging from a few individuals to several dozen. They are known for their synchronized swimming and diving behaviors. Narwhals are skilled divers, capable of reaching depths of over 4,000 feet (1,200 meters). They feed on a diet of fish and squid, using their echolocation abilities to locate prey.

Vocalizations: Narwhals communicate using a variety of vocalizations, including clicks, whistles, and pulsed sounds. These vocalizations are important for navigation, social interactions, and possibly in locating food in the dark Arctic waters.

Conservation Status: The conservation status of narwhals is currently listed as "Least Concern" by the International Union for Conservation of Nature (IUCN). However, they face potential threats from climate change, which can impact their Arctic habitat, as well as human activities such as shipping, oil and gas development, and potential disturbances from increased human presence in their environment.

Cultural Significance: Narwhals hold cultural significance in Inuit communities, where they are valued for their meat, skin, and tusks. The narwhal tusk has also been the subject of various myths and legends, and in medieval times, it was even believed to be the horn of the mythical unicorn.

In summary, the narwhal is an iconic Arctic species with its unique tusk and adaptations to life in icy waters. While they are currently not considered endangered, ongoing research and conservation efforts are essential to monitor potential threats and ensure the continued well-being of these remarkable marine mammals.

MENTAL BOMB

Our goal is to entertain and to blow your mind!

Visit us online at MentalBomb.com
Home for the best illusions, riddles, games, and fun facts!

Follow

Facebook:	Mental-Bomb-
Instagram:	mental_bomb_
Pinterest:	Mental_Bomb
Twitter:	MentalBomb_

www.ingramcontent.com/pod-product-compliance
Lightning Source LLC
Chambersburg PA
CBHW061016260726
48661CB00005B/2208